Discover Horses

by Katrina Streza

© 2017 by Katrina Streza
ISBN: 978-1-53240-240-1
eISBN: 978-1-53240-241-8
Images licensed from Fotolia.com
All rights reserved.
No portion of this book may be reproduced
without express permission of the publisher.
First Edition
Published in the United States by
Xist Publishing
www.xistpublishing.com
PO Box 61593 Irvine, CA 92602

There are many different kinds of horses.

3

4

Horses like to run and jump.

This is a show horse.
She is jumping.

8

This horse is a boy.
He is a stallion.

This horse is a girl.
She is a mare.

This is a baby horse.
It is a foal.

13

This horse has spots.
It is an Appaloosa.

15

This horse has a pretty walk. It is a Friesian.

This horse is strong.
It is a Comtois.

This horse is very strong.
It is a Clydesdale.

This horse can run.
It is a Thoroughbred.

23

This is a smart horse.
It is an Arabian.

25

This is a beautiful horse. It is an Andalusian.

This is not a horse.
It is a pony.

29

30

This is not a horse.
It is a donkey.

This is not a horse.
It is a zebra.